Twenty to Make
Mini Gift Boxes

Michelle Powell

Search Press

D0279987

First published in Great Britain 2009

Search Press Limited
Wellwood, North Farm Road,
Tunbridge Wells, Kent TN2 3DR

Reprinted 2011, 2012

Text copyright © Michelle Powell 2009

Photographs by Debbie Patterson at
Search Press Studios

Photographs and design copyright
© Search Press Ltd 2009

Print ISBN: 978-1-84448-462-1
Epub ISBN: 978-1-78126-015-9
Mobi ISBN: 978-1-78126-070-8
PDF ISBN: 978-1-78126-124-8

Suppliers
If you have difficulty in obtaining any of the
materials and equipment mentioned in this book,
then please visit the Search Press website for
details of suppliers: www.searchpress.com

Printed in Malaysia

Dedication
This book is for Phoebe Mae,
with all my love always.

Contents

Introduction

Making your own gift box or bag really does add a special finishing touch when gift giving. It allows you to personalise the gift, theme the box to match the occasion or simply add a touch of luxury! So often we give impersonal gifts such as money or vouchers, particularly for special occasions, and a beautiful, hand-made gift box can turn it into something really special.

Although all the creations in this book are fully functioning gift boxes, they could easily be used as papercraft sculptures, seasonal decorations, party favour boxes or as really special three-dimensional greetings cards. The boxes shown are 'mini', but all the designs can be scaled up to make a larger box if required.

There are many ways to make boxes so I've tried to incorporate a selection in this book. Quick and simple projects just involve decorating a pre-purchased box; often wedding favour boxes are ideal to be used in this way. Some boxes are made using die cutters or personal cutting machines and decorated with punches; these will speed up the job if you have them, but are not essential. You can easily hand-cut the box net yourself using a template, or by opening out a small food-packing box and drawing around the edges. Alternatively, use ready-made box blanks.

Many of the boxes here are created using folding techniques, and the dimensions are given in this book so that these boxes can be created from scratch. Try a simple origami box such as the one on page 14 (ingeniously made from a square of paper without the need for any cutting or gluing), make a mini pram for a new baby or even create a chocolate cake guaranteed to be calorie free!

I hope you enjoy making the creations in this book as much as I did, and make the gifts for your friends and loved-ones really special.

Templates and guides

All of the templates are reproduced at half their actual size. They should therefore be photocopied at 200 per cent. The cutting and folding guides on page 7 are not drawn to scale.

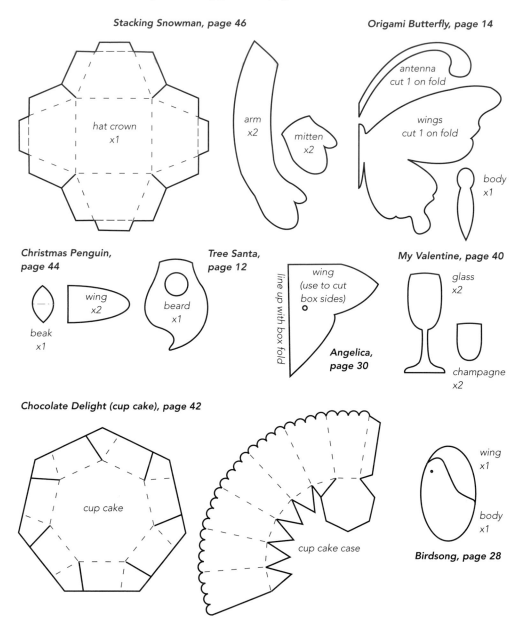

Stacking Snowman, page 46

hat crown
x1

arm
x2

mitten
x2

Origami Butterfly, page 14

antenna
cut 1 on fold

wings
cut 1 on fold

body
x1

Christmas Penguin, page 44

beak
x1

wing
x2

Tree Santa, page 12

beard
x1

line up with box fold

wing
(use to cut box sides)

Angelica, page 30

My Valentine, page 40

glass
x2

champagne
x2

Chocolate Delight (cup cake), page 42

cup cake

cup cake case

wing
x1

body
x1

Birdsong, page 28

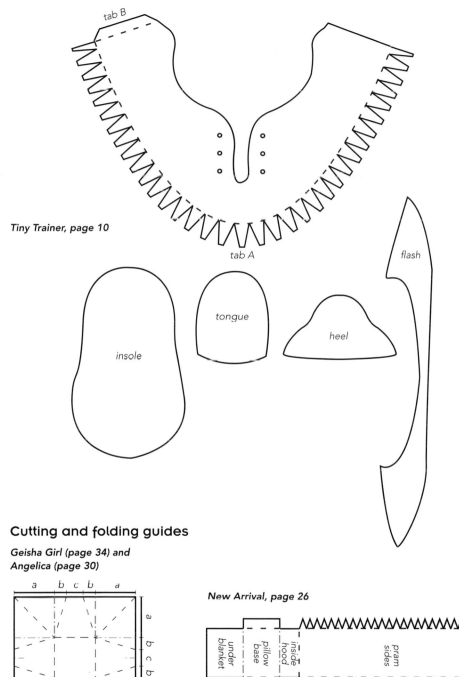

tab B

Tiny Trainer, page 10

tab A

flash

tongue

heel

insole

Cutting and folding guides

Geisha Girl (page 34) and
Angelica (page 30)

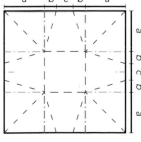

a   b   c   b   a

a
b
c
b
a

New Arrival, page 26

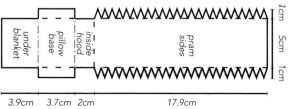

under blanket

pillow base

inside hood

pram sides

1cm
5cm
1cm

3.9cm   3.7cm   2cm   17.9cm

Torn and Twisted

Materials:
Patterned card
Lemon, pale green, blue and brown card
Brown cord
All-purpose glue
3D foam pads

Tools:
Circle punch, 2.5cm (1in)
Flower punch
Ball-tipped embossing stylus and foam pad
Craft knife and cutting mat

Instructions:

1 Cut a 20cm (7¾in) square of patterned card, and score a line 8cm (3¼in) from each edge. Score diagonally through each of the corner squares now visible, scoring from the centre to the outside edge. The 4cm (1½in) square formed in the centre is the box base.

2 Fold up the sides of the box so that the folded corner triangles stick out. Fold each triangle over on to the next side, and the point on around again to the next side and glue for a twisted look.

3 Tear a rough circle shape about 7.5cm (3in) in diameter from lemon card. Tear in to the circle five times to create petals. Don't try to make it too regular. Curl each petal and scrunch up the flower.

4 Repeat, tearing a circle of pale green card about 6.5cm (2½in) in diameter. Punch a 2.5cm (1in) circle of blue card and a smaller brown flower shape. Cup the flower using an embossing stylus.

5 Cut four 7cm (2¾in) lengths of brown cord, knot each end and glue them across the blue circle. Fix the cupped flower on top using 3D foam pads. Assemble the bloom using 3D foam pads.

6 For the lid, cut a 7.5cm (3in) square of blue card and score a line 1.5cm (⅝in) from each side. Cut along one of the score lines on each side, as far as the central square. Tear the edge on each side.

7 Fold on the score lines and glue the small tabs behind the lid sides to assemble. Attach the torn bloom to the top of the lid using 3D foam pads.

Back to Nature

The organic, loose shape of this flower really suits earthy, natural colours, so it looks wonderful in browns, reds and greens. Choose your patterned card for the box itself, then match the plain card colours to it to create the coordinating torn bloom.

To create a matching tag, tear a second flower starting with circles roughly 6cm (2¼in) and 5cm (2in) in diameter. Add a 1.8cm (¾in) circle and a 1.5cm (⅝in) flower to the centre. Mount on a 7.5cm (3in) circle of card, with matching cord to hang.

9

Tiny Trainer

Materials:

Templates: shoe, heel, flash, tongue and insole (page 7)

Blue and white card

Fine white cord

All-purpose glue

Tools:

Craft knife and cutting mat

Small hole punch

Perforating tool

Scissors

Instructions:

1 Use the templates on page 7 to cut out the shoe and heel from white card and the flash, tongue and insole from blue card.

2 Punch the lace holes, then score and fold where shown on the template. Use a perforating tool to add faux stitching to the edges of some pieces. Cut 50cm (19¾in) of cord and lace up the shoe loosely.

3 Starting at the centre front of the shoe, line up tab A with the front of the insole. Glue tab A to the underside of the insole so that the tab is visible on the outside of the shoe.

4 Continue gluing the small tabs to the insole on both sides of the shoe. Make sure all the tabs are visible on the outside of the sole. Overlap the flap (tab B) at the back and glue.

5 Glue the flash to the sides of the shoe and the heel to the back to cover the join. Glue the base of the tongue inside the shoe behind the holes. Tighten up the laces and tie in a bow.

6 Cut a rectangle of white card slightly larger than the base of the shoe. Apply glue to the shoe base and the exposed tabs and stick to the rectangle. When dry, use scissors to trim closely around the edge of the shoe to finish off.

Punch a circle of white card to make a matching tag. Decorate with a flash of blue card and more faux stitching. Use the same cord as for the laces to hang the tag.

Bonny Bootee

Create a yellow alternative to the Tiny Trainer.
Use the same templates as before, but trim away the lace holes in a
curved shape and trim off the arched shaping at the heel sides. Cut a
strip of card 5.5 x 1.5cm (2⅛ x ⅝in) to use as a strap. Add a punched
flower, a large brad and rickrack to finish the shoe.

Tree Santa

Materials:

Template: beard (page 6)

Red, white, flesh-coloured and lime card

White organza ribbon

Red self-adhesive gemstone

Pink chalks

All-purpose glue

3D foam pads

Tools:

Cricut machine with 'bags, tags, boxes and more' cartridge

Large flower punch

Circle punches, 2cm (¾in), 1.3cm (⅝in) and 0.6cm (¼in)

Small holly die cutter

Ball-tipped embossing stylus and foam mat

Craft knife and cutting mat

Scissors

Draw around the assembled box to create a triangle-shaped tag. Add a Santa face, as for the box, to create a fun gift tag. Team with a parcel wrapped in plain green paper for a coordinated look.

Instructions:

1 Use a Cricut machine to cut a wedge-shaped box approx. 7.5 x 5cm (3 x 2in) from red card. Alternatively use a ready-made box or bought template to create the box.

2 Assemble the box and punch holes at either side of the point. Thread through 25cm (9¾in) of ribbon and knot on the inside.

3 Cut two circles of flesh-coloured card 2cm (¾in) and 0.6cm (¼in) in diameter. Using a ball-tipped embossing tool, burnish the small circle (nose) on the back to cup the shape. Punch two tiny holes in the large circle for eyes and add chalk to the cheeks and mouth area.

4 Use the template to cut a beard shape from white card. Also punch a large flower shape and a 1.3cm (⅝in) diameter circle from white card.

5 Cut two petals from the punched white flower and bend to create a moustache. Assemble the face and beard using 3D foam pads. Add a die- or hand-cut holly leaf and gemstone berry.

6 Stick the Santa face to the box using 3D foam pads. Cup the remaining white circle using an embossing tool as for the nose and stick to the box top using a 3D foam pad.

Merlin's Magic

For a Hallowe'en or magic-themed party, transform Santa into Merlin! Cut the box from purple card and add stars cut or punched from iridescent paper. Cut the beard and moustache from grey card to complete the transformation. This design could also be adapted to make three wise men.

Origami Butterfly

Materials:

Templates: butterfly wings, antenna and body (page 6)

Floral patterned paper

Plain blue paper

Gold print card

Sage green and gold-coloured card

Gold cord

All-purpose glue

3D foam pads

Tools:

Craft knife and cutting mat

Scissors

Instructions:

1 Begin with the box lid. Cut a 25cm (9¾in) square of floral patterned paper and find the centre by folding diagonally point to point both ways. Open out flat and place face down.

2 Fold all four corners into the centre point to create a smaller square. Rotate slightly so that it is aligned like a square, not a diamond. Leave folded.

3 Fold the lower edge horizontally up so that it meets the centre point. Fold the upper edge horizontally down to meet the centre point. Unfold both folds.

Round the corners on a 5.5 x 10cm (2⅛ x 4in) card rectangle and add a square hole reinforcer and a punched butterfly to make a quick and simple matching tag.

4 Rotate the piece 90° and repeat step 3 so that the other two sides also have fold creases; remember to unfold these last two folds.

5 Unfold the left and right sides. Then, refold the top and bottom edges to the centre, creating a long narrow shape with a diamond at each end.

6 Place your fingernail at the top right corner of the centre square, which will form the base of the box (defined by fold lines), and fold the top right-hand edge down so that the point of the diamond faces vertically down. Unfold and repeat, folding up from the bottom, then unfold. Repeat both folds on the other end, remembering to unfold.

7 Partially unfold the top and bottom sides so that they stand up vertically. Pull up the points of the diamond on each side to create the third and fourth sides of the box. Make sure the corners of the box fold inwards as you do so.

8 Fold the extra vertical paper down inside the box and along the base so that the point returns to its original central position. Repeat on the other end.

9 For the box itself, cut a 24.3cm (9½in) square of plain blue paper (0.7mm, or ¼in, smaller than the first), and fold in the same way.

10 Put the lid on the box and tie with cord. Use the templates on page 6 to cut out a butterfly from gold print (wings), sage green (antennae) and gold-coloured (body) card. Assemble using 3D foam pads and attach to the box.

Winged Beauty

Use bright shades of denim blue, terracotta and white for a bold variation on this box design. Just make your butterfly to match the colours of the paper used to ensure perfect colour coordination.

Ladybug, Ladybug

Materials:

Round papier-mâché box, 5cm (2in)

Black poster paint

Red flock spotted card

Black glitter card

Yellow card

Red self-adhesive gemstone

Black chenille stick

All-purpose glue

3D foam pads

Tools:

Circle punches, 7.5cm (3in) and 3.5cm (1⅜in)

Flower punch, 3cm (1¼in)

Craft knife and cutting mat

Small paintbrush

Wire cutters

Tip!

An easy way to cut a punched circle in half is to punch another circle from scrap paper and fold this in half. Line it up with the edges of the card circle and mark the fold position.

Make a quick and simple gift tag using a 5cm (2in) punched circle for the body and a 2.5cm (1in) circle for the head. Cut 4cm (1½in) into the body and glue, overlapping the cut points to create a very shallow cone. Mount on a 7.5cm (3in) circle of card with grass and a flower decoration.

Instructions:

1 Paint the round papier-mâché box with black paint and leave to dry. Punch a 7.5cm (3in) diameter circle from red spotted card and cut the circle in half to create two wings.

2 Overlap the two wings about 2.5cm (1in) at one end to create an open triangle shape in between. Glue the two half-circles together. Leave the other end open for now.

3 Punch a 3.5cm (1⅜in) circle from black glitter card and glue it under the overlapped wings so that only one-third of the circle protrudes.

4 Cut 20cm (7¾in) of black chenille stick, bend in half and curl the ends to create antennae. Glue under the bug's head. Apply glue around the edge of the front part of the box lid and glue on the head end of the ladybug.

5 When the glue has dried, bend the wing tips so that they overlap and glue to the side of the box lid, forcing the wings to create a curved body shape.

6 Punch a 3cm (1¼in) flower shape from yellow card. Bend the petals with your fingers to shape and add a gemstone to the centre. Attach this to the ladybug's head to finish.

Gardener's Delight
Alter the colours to lilac, pink and lime green to make a very colourful bug. These boxes would make ideal party favours for a child's birthday. Try also reversing the positions of the wings and adding a body to create a butterfly version of this box.

Designer Daisy

Materials:

Raspberry-coloured, white and pale pink card

Striped black and white paper

Black cord

Large black brad

All-purpose glue

3D foam pads

Tools:

Die-cutting machine with purse-style box and flower dies

Flower stamen punch

Ball-tipped embossing stylus and foam mat

Craft knife and cutting mat

Scissors

Instructions:

1 Use a die-cutting machine to cut a purse shape from raspberry-coloured card. Fold the box on the score lines and glue in the side pieces. Alternatively use a ready-made box or bought template to create the box.

2 Cut a 3cm (1¼in) strip of striped black and white paper and glue to the box flap, gluing the excess to the small top section and back of the box.

3 Use the die cutter or a punch to cut a large daisy shape from white card. Burnish on the back of each petal using a ball-tipped embossing tool to add curve. Turn the flower over and burnish in the centre to lift the petals up.

4 Punch two flower stamen shapes from pale pink card. Burnish in the centre of one and glue on top of the second. Use a large black brad to assemble the flower.

5 Cut 70cm (27½in) of black cord and tie in a bow around the centre of the box. Knot and trim the ends. Attach the flower to the box using 3D foam pads.

Decorate a special gift with a bloom and tag. Make the flower in the same way as for the box and attach a cord bow and a triangle-shaped tag decorated with a strip of striped paper.

Giant Gerbera

This stylish design will work in any colour combination, such as the brown and blue shown here. Add a ribbon handle to the box rather than the cord to create a handbag-style box.

Tip!
If the cord you use to wrap around the box is chunky, the box won't sit straight on its base. To combat this, add two small 3D foam pad feet to either side of the box base so that it stands beautifully.

Winter Wreath

Materials:

Round papier-mâché box, 7cm (2¾in)
Turquoise poster paint
Turquoise and white glitter card
Lime green card
9 silver beads
Green wire, 80cm (31½in)
White organza ribbon, 60cm (23½in)
All-purpose glue
3D foam pads

Tools:

Circle punch, 7.5cm (3in)
Flower punch
Holly leaf punch
Leaf sprig punch
Ball-tipped embossing stylus and
    foam mat
Craft knife and cutting mat
Small paintbrush
Wire cutters
Scissors

Instructions:

1 Paint the papier-mâché box with turquoise paint and leave to dry. Wrap the organza ribbon around the box base and tie in a bow at the front.

2 Punch or hand-cut a 7.5cm (3in) diameter circle of turquoise glitter card and glue to the box lid.

3 Punch or hand-cut fourteen holly leaves from green card and six leaf sprigs from white glitter card. Score down the centre of each and fold slightly to give dimension.

4 Cut five flower shapes from white glitter card for the fir cone. Burnish each in the middle using the ball-tipped embossing tool to cup the shapes and bend the tip of each petal back with your fingers.

5 Cut into the centre of one of the flower shapes and roll up tightly to create the centre of the fir cone. Glue in the centre of another flower shape. Use a single small 3D foam pad to attach the remaining three flower shapes to give height to the fir cone.

6 Thread nine silver beads on to the green wire, twisting the wire after each bead to secure. Attach to the top of the box using three 3D foam pads, then attach the holly, leaf sprigs and fir cone using 3D foam pads to cover the wire.

The tiny box is ideal for hanging on the tree or decorating the Christmas table. Decorate the top of a 4cm (1½in) cube box with two holly leaves, two wired bead berries, a leaf sprig and fir cone. Add a loop of ribbon to hang. Add a 1.5cm (⅝in) strip of glitter card around the box sides.

Festive Fun

Create a more traditional Christmas look by using the classic colours of deep green, rich red and brown. The Christmas wreath is so iconic, you can alter the colours to virtually anything and it will still look like a holly wreath. Try black and silver or turquoise and copper for some really modern alternatives.

Retro Style

Materials:

Black pillow box,
  11 x 8 x 3cm (4¼ x
  3¼ x 1¼in)

Turquoise, burgundy
  and pink card

Dark burgundy
  ribbon, 18cm (7in)

Large black brad

All-purpose glue

3D foam pads

Tools:

Circle punch,
  5cm (2in)

Retro flower punch,
  4.5cm (1¾in)

Flower stamen punch

Craft knife and
  cutting mat

Scissors

Instructions:

1 Use a ready-made bought pillow box or
use a pillow box template to cut your own.
Assemble the box.

2 Punch or hand-cut a 5cm (2in) circle of
turquoise card. Attach it to one side of the
pillow box using all-purpose glue.

3 Wrap ribbon around the pillow box, gluing
one end just beyond the top edge of the box,
then fold over the other end of the ribbon and
glue neatly on top.

4 Punch a 4.5cm (1¾in) retro flower from
burgundy card. Punch a stamen from pink card
and attach to the centre of the flower using a
3D foam pad.

5 Cut a small slit through the centre of the
stamen and push through a large black brad
and fix. Attach the flower to the pillow box
using 3D foam pads so that it sits in the centre
of the circle.

Disco Glamour

Team funky purple glitter card with cool lime green to create a totally 70s glam version of this design. For a more subtle design try using red on the flower with a green backing circle on a straw yellow box to create a poppy-field look.

Create a small round box ideal for a gift of jewellery or money. Paint a 5cm (2in) round papier-mâché box black and add a retro flower motif as for the pillow box. Wrap ribbon around the box sides.

Pretty in Purple

Materials:

Blue patterned card

Purple and
turquoise card

Blue cord

Wide purple
organza ribbon

Gemstone brad

Blue glitter

All-purpose glue

3D foam pads

Fine glue pen

Tools:

Die-cutting machine
with handbag-
shaped die

Flower punch,
5cm (2in)

Circle punch,
1.3cm (⅝in)

Hole punch

Craft knife and
cutting mat

Scissors

Instructions:

1 Use a die cutter to cut a handbag-shaped box from patterned blue card. Score and fold where shown. Alternatively use one of the many handbag-shaped box templates available to buy.

2 Punch two holes in the top of the bag. Cut 17cm (6¾in) of blue cord, thread through the holes and knot separately inside. Glue the knots to the inside of the box so that the cord handle stands upright.

3 Use a fine glue pen to add a line of blue glitter to the lower edge of the flap. When dry, glue the tabs to assemble the box.

4 Punch three purple flowers, score down the centre of each petal and fold. Layer the flowers and glue. Punch a 1.3cm (⅝in) circle of turquoise card and attach to the flower centre using a gemstone brad.

5 Cut 40cm (15¾in) of wide organza ribbon and tie in a bow around the right-hand side of the cord handle. Attach the flower to the front of the bag using 3D foam pads.

Use a punch to create a large tag from patterned card and add a punched flower made as for the gift box. Finish the tag with a dash of gorgeous purple organza ribbon.

Springtime Treat

This cute handbag is sure to be adored by girls young and old! Soft shades of sage green and creamy yellow create a more grown-up look, or use hot pink, yellow and white for a little girl's gift box.

New Arrival

Materials:

Cutting and folding guide
(page 7)

Pink dotty card

Purple dotty card

Flesh-coloured, white, light
brown and lavender card

Pink self-adhesive gemstones

White chenille stick

Pink narrow organza ribbon

Chalks

All-purpose glue

3D foam pads

Tools:

Circle punches, 7.5cm (3in),
2.5cm (1in), 1.5cm (⅝in) and
0.7cm (¼in)

Medium and small
daisy punches

Small flower punch

Small tag punch

Spiral punch

Small hole punch

Scalloped scissors

Ball-tipped embossing stylus
and foam mat

Craft knife and cutting mat

Scissors

*Make a matching tag with a mini baby face made from
1.9cm (¾in) and 0.4cm (¼in) punched circles. Mount the
head on a 3.5cm (1⅜in) daisy shape, on a 3.7cm (1⅜in)
circle and finally on a 5cm (2in) scalloped circle.*

Instructions:

1 Punch or hand-cut two 7.5cm (3in) circles from pink dotty card. Cut into the centre, then fold back one quarter from each circle to create the sides of the pram. Cut a strip of pink dotty card following the cutting and folding guide on page 7, and fold where shown.

2 Starting at the handle position, glue the triangular tabs of the long strip to one pram side, curving as you go, and repeat for the second side. Unfold the quarter circle flaps from the pram pieces and glue over the tabs to neaten.

3 Fold the 'inside hood' flap inside the box, lining the front part of the hood. Glue the 'pillow base' flap diagonally so that the 'under blanket' flap sits horizontally.

4 Cut a 7.2 x 5cm (2¾ x 2in) rectangle of purple dotty card. Score 1cm (½in) from the edge on three sides (two short and one long) and fold. Round the corners and glue to the 'under blanket' flap.

5 Punch a 2.5cm (1in) and two 0.7cm (¼in) circles for the baby head and ears from flesh-coloured card. Punch holes for the eyes, cut a mouth and nose and chalk the cheeks. Add sections of punched light brown card spirals for the hair.

6 Cut a 4.5 x 3.5cm (1¾ x 1⅜in) white card rectangle using scalloped scissors to create the pillow. Assemble the head and attach to the pillow. Glue inside the box.

7 Punch and layer 2.5cm (1in) and 1.5cm (⅝in) circles of card to create the wheels and decorate each with a gemstone centre. Cut 18cm (7in) of chenille stick and bend into a handle shape. Glue the ends to the underside of the blanket.

8 Punch two daisy shapes, curve the petals with a ball-tipped embossing tool and add a self-adhesive gemstone to each centre. Attach to the box with 3D foam pads. Punch a tiny tag, decorate with a punched flower and hang from the handle using pink organza ribbon.

Baby in Blue
The blanket on this cute baby pram lifts to reveal the inside of the box. Alter the colours to pastel blues and greens for a baby boy or make it in shades of cream and brown for a modern look.

Birdsong

Materials:

Templates: bird body/wing (optional)
(page 6)

Floral patterned paper

Plain mauve paper

Green dotty card

Olive green, yellow and mauve
coloured card

Raffia

Cream eyelet

Chalks

Fine black pen

All-purpose glue

3D foam pads

Tools:

Circle punch, 5cm (2in)

Oval punch, 5.5 x 3cm (2⅛ x 1¼in)

Small hole punch

Tiny hole punch

Craft knife and cutting mat

Eyelet setting tool and hammer

Scissors

Make a mini box by folding a box base from a 15.3cm (6in) square and a lid from a 16cm (6¼in) square. Decorate with a bird made as for the larger box mounted on a punched scalloped square.

Instructions:

1 Make a box following the instructions on pages 14–15 (Origami Butterfly). Use a 20cm (7¾in) square of floral patterned paper for the lid, and exactly the same size of plain mauve paper for the base.

2 Cut a strip of mauve card 30 x 6.5cm (11¾ x 2½in). Fold every 7cm (2¾in) along its length and glue inside the box base, lining the sides to extend them higher so that the box lid can sit on top.

3 Punch a 5cm (2in) circle of mauve card. Punch a hole near the edge of the circle and inset a cream eyelet using a setting tool and hammer.

4 Punch a 5.5 x 3cm (2⅛ x 1¼in) oval out of green dotty card and trim off the top in a curve to create a bird shape following the template on page 6. Use the trimmed-off piece as a template for the wing. Draw around it on to olive green card and cut out.

5 Cut a triangle of yellow card for the beak, punch a tiny hole for the eye and chalk the cheek. Use a fine black pen to add dashed lines around the wing, body, beak and circle tag.

6 Cut some raffia strands 7cm (2¾in) long, knot in the centre and trim off the strands on one side close to the knot. Glue the knot to the back of the bird body to create the tail.

7 Assemble the tag using glue and 3D foam pads. Cut some raffia strands 60cm (23½in) long, tie around the box and trim to the desired length. Tie the tag to the box using a single raffia strand.

Blue Bird

This box is so versatile it could be made in any colour scheme; in this case cream and duck egg blue create a warm country look. Vary the colours used to create a Christmas robin or Easter chick variation.

Angelica

Materials:

Cutting and folding
guide (page 7)

Template: wing
(page 6)

White, flesh-coloured
and yellow card

Pale blue glitter card

Sage dotty card

Silver mirri card

Narrow blue ribbon

Silver-coloured wire

Chalks

White glitter

All-purpose glue

3D foam pads

Tools:

Circle punches,
2.5cm (1in) and
3.8cm (1½in)

Scalloped square
punch, 3.7cm (1⅜in)

Large flower punch

Small hole punch

Tiny hole punch

Heart punch

Star punch

Craft knife and
cutting mat

Scissors

Pliers

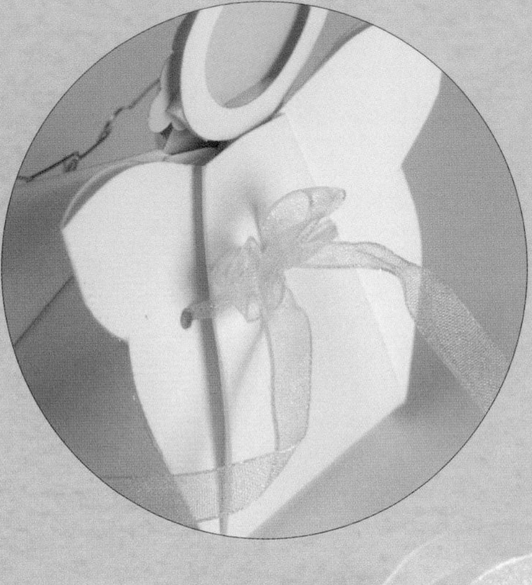

*Make an angel tag for a regular wrapped
gift. Make a head as for the box and attach
it to a wedge-shaped tag 7cm (2¾in) long,
5cm (2in) wide at the base and 3cm (1¼in)
wide at the top.*

Instructions:

1 Using the cutting and folding guide on page 7, cut a 17cm (6¾in) square of white card and score lines so that distance (a) is 6cm (2¼in), (b) is 1.5cm (⅝in) and (c) is 2cm (¾in).

2 Fold the score lines as shown. Fold into a rough pyramid shape, with an extra folded triangle flap of card protruding at each corner.

3 Using the wing template on page 6, trim the back two triangular flaps into wings, cutting both layers at once, and punch the marked holes. Also punch holes in the front two triangles and bend forwards and down to shape the sleeves.

4 Cut the box front into a V-shaped neckline between the two sleeves. Cut 40cm (15¾in) of ribbon and thread through all four holes, tying it loosely at the back.

5 Add a line of glitter to the neck, wing edges and sleeve edge. When dry, glue the sleeves into place. Cut a 2 x 1.5cm (¾ x ⅝in) rectangle of flesh-coloured card for the neck.

6 Punch a 2.5cm (1in) circle for the face and add punched eyes, a cut nose and mouth and chalked cheeks. Punch a 3.7cm (1⅜in) scalloped square from yellow card, fold over 1.3cm (⅝in) for a fringe and round the folded corners to create hair.

7 Assemble the head and neck using 3D foam pads and glue to the dress behind the neckline. Punch a large flower from flesh-coloured card and cut off two petals for the hands. Punch a small hole in each hand.

8 Use 3.8cm (1½in) and 2.5cm (1in) diameter circle punches to create a halo from silver mirri card and glue to the back of the head. Cut 16cm (6¼in) of wire and thread on two punched shapes made from pale blue glitter card and sage dotty card. Bend the wire then attach either end through the holes in the hands. Glue the hands inside the sleeves.

Gabriel

Use warm shades of gold, brown and green to create a country-style angel complete with her hanging red star and green heart. This angel would also look stunning made entirely in silver mirri card, for a really modern feel.

Fish 'n' Gifts

Materials:

White card

Turquoise, lime and sea green glitter card

Turquoise dotty paper

Orange dotty flock card

Orange ribbon

Turquoise brad

All-purpose glue

3D foam pads

Tools:

Circle punches, 1.3cm (⅝in), 2.5cm (1in) and 3.7cm (1⅜in)

Retro flower punch

Heart punch

Large hole punch

Tiny hole punch

Cricut machine with 'bags, tags, boxes and more' cartridge

Craft knife and cutting mat

Wavy scissors

Scissors

Use a larger fish decoration to decorate the top of a small, round box. Use the same double-punching technique that you used for creating the leaf shape to make a crescent for the face. A 5cm (2in) circle punch is used for both the body and crescent, and a leaf-shaped punch makes a great fin.

32

Instructions:

1 Use a Cricut machine to cut a bag shape 7.5 x 2.8 x 2.5cm (3 x 1¼ x 1in) from turquoise dotty paper. Assemble the bag and glue the base. Alternatively use a ready-made bag or bought template to create the bag. Cut along the top edges with wavy scissors.

2 Punch two 2.5cm (1in) circles from sea green glitter card and stick one on either side at the top of the bag. Cut a piece of ribbon 15cm (6in) long, fold in half and attach to the top of the bag using a brad through both punched circles.

3 Punch a 3.7cm (1⅜in) circle from turquoise glitter card and a retro flower shape from orange dotty flock card. Use 3D foam pads to attach the circle off-centre on the flower so that the petals look like fins.

4 Punch a 3.7cm (1⅜in) circle from sea green glitter card then punch it again to trim it to a leaf shape. Punch a 1.3cm (⅝in) circle of white card for the eye and punch a tiny hole to one side.

5 Punch a heart shape from orange dotty card and attach it to the back of the leaf-shaped piece. Stick to the left of the circle. Attach the eye using 3D foam pads.

6 Punch a heart from lime glitter card for the lips and attach behind the turquoise circle.

7 Cut a tag shape 9 x 3.7cm (3½ x 1⅜in) from white card, punch a large hole in the top and stick it to the front of the bag. Attach the fish to the tag.

Fishing for Compliments

Fish come in such a beautiful array of colours you can really let your imagination run wild and create a fish in any colour you like. This pink dot, purple glitter and green flock fish is certainly imaginary!

Geisha Girl

Materials:

Cutting and folding guide
  (page 7)

Blue and gold washi origami
  paper, 20 x 20cm (7¾ x 7¾in)

White, flesh-coloured, black
  and blue card

Gold crinkle paper

Narrow white ribbon

Silver self-adhesive gemstone

Chalks

All-purpose glue

3D foam pads

Tools:

Circle punches, 1.5cm (⅝in),
  2.5cm (1in) and 3.8cm (1½in)

Postage stamp punch

Small flower punch

Tiny hole punch

Craft knife and cutting mat

Scissors

Instructions:

1 Using the guide on page
7, cut a 19cm (7½in) square of
origami paper and score the
lines so that distance (a) is 7cm
(2¾in), (b) is 1cm (½in) and (c)
is 3cm (1¼in).

2 Fold the score lines as
shown. Fold into a rough
pyramid shape, with an extra
folded triangle flap of card
protruding at each corner.

3 Bend the right-hand front
triangle forwards on to the
front face of the box, angling
the point down slightly so that
the lower side of the flap now
runs horizontally across the
front of the box and the point
is touching the left-hand join.

Squash to create a fold in the flap and repeat on the left side.

4 Fold the remaining protruding part of the flap over again so that it lies flat on the first, creating one side of the kimono front. Repeat on the other side. You may need to trim the points of the first fold slightly so that they sit neatly.

5 Punch a hole in the centre front and back near the neckline. Cut 40cm (15¾in) of ribbon, thread through both holes and tie loosely at the back. Fold the back two flaps forward so that the top edges line up with the top fold of the front flaps. Fold the points over and glue.

6 Cut a strip of blue card 1 x 3.5cm (½ x 1⅜in) and glue on as a waistband. Cut a 2cm (¾in) square of flesh-coloured card for the neck and cut a V-shaped notch in a second white 2cm (¾in) square for the vest.

7 Punch a 2.5cm (1in) circle for the face, add punched eyes, a cut nose and mouth and chalk the cheeks and lips.

8 Punch two 3.8cm (1½in) circles from black card. Use a postage stamp punch to punch a section from one circle, and trim off the postage perforations at the sides, leaving them at the top to create a fringe.

9 Punch a 1.5cm (⅝in) circle from black card, a flower from blue card and a rectangle of gold crinkle paper 1.6 x 0.6cm (⅝ x ¼in). Assemble the head, hair and neck using 3D foam pads and glue to the kimono behind the V neckline.

Kandy Kimono

Washi origami paper is ideal for this project as the designs are based on kimono prints. The soft foldable paper seems to have a fabric-like quality. So many beautiful printed washi papers are available you could create many variations of this box.

Use the simple origami fold on pages 14–15 to create a mini matching gift box, with a cherry blossom punched tag. Start with a 16cm (6¼in) square for the lid and a 15.3cm (6in) square for the base.

Born to Shop

Materials:

Brown, cream, yellow, mid and pale blue card

Sage dotty card

Blue and yellow brads

White pen

All-purpose glue

3D foam pads

Tools:

Circle punches, 1.5cm (⅝in), 1.8cm (¾in), 2.5cm (1in) and 3.8cm (1½in) in diameter

Dot embossing folder and die-cutting machine

Flower punch

Daisy punch

Bloom punch

Single needle perforating tool

Ball-tipped embossing stylus

Craft knife and cutting mat

Cut a circle with a diameter of 6.5cm (2½in) to create a matching tag. Decorate with a mini handle, made from circles 2.7cm (1in) and 1.6cm (⅝in) in diameter, punched flowers and more faux stitching.

Instructions:

1 Cut a rectangle of brown card 29 x 10cm (11½ x 4in). Score a line 3cm (1¼in) away from one of the long sides. Starting from one end of a long side, score lines at 3cm (1¼in), 13cm (5in), 16cm (6¼in) and 26cm (10¼in), which should leave a 3cm (1¼in) section at the end.

2 Fold on the score lines to create a bag shape. Cut through the tab at each corner of the bag so the base will fold.

3 Punch a 2.5cm (1in) circular hole in a piece of brown card, then punch a second 3.8cm (1½in) hole around it to make a ring of card for the bag handle. Repeat to make a second.

4 Glue the handles in position on the front and back of the bag, and trim the excess bag inside the circle handles away.

5 Draw the flower stems and faux stitch lines on the bag and handle using a white pen. Use the perforating tool to add a hole at the end of each drawn stitch.

6 Punch five flower shapes from coloured card, and five circular flower centres. Place two of the centres in the dot embossing folder and run through a die-cutting machine to emboss.

7 Burnish some of the flowers and centres on the back using a ball-tipped embossing tool. Add brads to two flower centres and assemble the flowers. Stick in place on the bag using 3D foam pads.

Pretty in Pastels

Pretty shades of pink, lemon and lavender give a fun, spring-like feel to this gift bag. Remember to wrap your gift in lashings of pink tissue to complete the look.

Floral Treasures

Materials:

Green dotty chest-shaped box,
7 x 5 x 4.5cm (2¾ x 2 x 1¾in)

Cream glitter card

Brown, green and white card

White organza ribbon

All-purpose glue

3D foam pads

Tools:

Daisy punch, 3.5cm (1⅜in)

Flower stamen punch

Small flower punch

Leaf sprig punch

Ball-tipped embossing stylus
and foam mat

Die-cutting machine

Craft knife and cutting mat

Scissors

*Make a pretty tag decorated with a punched
glitter flower and leaf stem as for the gift
box. Add white organza ribbon to finish.*

Instructions:

1 Use a ready-made, bought 'treasure chest' box or use a box template to cut your own. Assemble the box.

2 Cut 50cm (19¾in) of white organza ribbon and wrap it around the box, tying in a bow at the top.

3 Punch two daisy flower shapes from cream glitter card. Burnish the back of each petal and the front centre of each flower using a ball-tipped embossing tool to give them dimension.

4 Punch a stamen shape from brown card and a small flower from white card. Burnish both in the centre to cup.

5 Glue the flowers on top of each other, rotating to give the appearance of more petals. Add the stamen then the flower centre, turning it over to create a domed effect.

6 Punch two leaf sprig shapes and use a die cutter (or hand-cut) to create a stem. Glue the leaves to the stem and tuck under the ribbon. Stick the flower in position using 3D foam pads.

Secret Wishes

White polka dots on a pink background create a feminine look for this floral box and tag. Make the flower from purple glitter card with hot pink stamen to complete the look.

My Valentine

Materials:

Templates: champagne glass
   and champagne (page 6)

Black, yellow and grey card

Burgundy dotty card

Black and grey spotty paper

Translucent-effect sheet

Wide burgundy organza ribbon

Iridescent glitter glue

Thread

Chalks

All-purpose glue

3D foam pads

Small, gold-coloured self-
   adhesive gemstones

Tools:

Heart punch

Circle punch, 1.8cm (¾in)

Tag punch, 8.5 x 4.5cm
   (3⅜ x 1¾in)

Craft knife and cutting mat

Scissors

*Make a matching 3.5cm (1⅜in)
cube box and decorate with
a 1.7cm (⅝in) strip of dotty
paper and a punched heart
motif. Ideal for an individual
Valentines chocolate or even
an engagement ring!*

Instructions:

1 Cut a rectangle of black card 11.5 x 9cm (4½ x 3½in). Score a line 1.5cm (⅝in) away from each side.

2 Where the two score lines cross at each corner, cut in on one of the two lines to create a tab. Repeat on all four corners and glue into a tray shape.

3 Cut a rectangle of burgundy dotty card 17 x 8.5cm (6¾ x 3⅜in). Wrap around the tray, folding at each corner. Use the remaining flap as a tab and glue to the other end to create a sleeve.

4 Use the templates to cut two champagne glasses from translucent-effect sheet and two champagnes from yellow card. Assemble the glasses and decorate with glitter glue and gold-coloured gemstones.

5 Punch a tag shape from black card and glue a 2cm (¾in) wide strip of black and grey spotty paper along the bottom edge. Punch a burgundy heart shape and attach to a circle of grey card with 3D foam pads. Chalk the edges.

6 Cut 65cm (25½in) of wide burgundy organza ribbon, wrap around the box and tie in a bow. Assemble the tag and tie it to the bow using a short piece of thread.

Gift of Love

This gift box is credit-card size, so perfect to beautifully package a modern gift voucher card for a wedding or christening gift. The white and soft pink colours could be varied to match the colour theme of the day.

Chocolate Delight

Materials:

Mid and dark brown, cream, burgundy and green card

Cream glitter card

Chalks

Brown glitter glue

All-purpose glue

3D foam pads

Tools:

Circle punch, 1.5cm (⅝in)

Flower punch

Daisy punch

Leaf punch

Cricut machine with 'bags, tags, boxes and more' cartridge

Ball-tipped embossing stylus

Craft knife and cutting mat

Instructions:

1 Use a Cricut machine to cut a wedge-shaped box 8.5 x 5.5 x 3.5cm (3⅜ x 2⅛ x 1⅜in) from mid brown card. Assemble the box and glue the point and side tabs. Alternatively, use a ready-made box or bought template to create the box.

2 Cut eight rectangles from dark brown card, roll them up tightly and glue to create 3.5cm (1⅜in) tall chocolate scrolls. Glue to the opening flap of the box. Add dots of glitter glue to the box top.

Make the most scrumptious matching cherry cup cake using the templates on page 6. For the pink icing, punch a 5cm (2in) scalloped circle and cut into the centre between two scallops. Overlap one scallop and glue creating a very shallow cone shape. Add a swirl of cream and a cherry as for the chocolate cake slice.

3 Cut a 1.5cm (⅝in) wide wavy strip of cream glitter card, 17.5cm (6⅞in) long, and a wavy burgundy card strip, about 0.7cm (¼in) wide. Glue to the sides of the box to look like cream and cherry filling.

4 Punch a daisy shape and a flower shape from cream card. Fold each of the petals on the daisy back, then over and stick to the flat flower shape using 3D foam pads to create a piped swirl of cream.

5 Punch two burgundy circles and trim a little to create a cherry shape. Hand-cut a cherry stem and punch a leaf from green card. Chalk the edges, and shape using a ball tipped embossing tool.

6 Assemble the cherry using a 3D foam pad in the centre to give dimension. Stick the cream swirl to the box using a 3D foam pad with the cherry on top.

Tip!

To make a mini carrot, use a single petal cut from a large punched daisy for the carrot, and a small lime-coloured punched flower, with all the petals scrunched together, for the carrot top.

Teatime Treat

Vary the colours to create a yummy carrot cake, complete with cream cheese frosting and mini paper version of the marzipan carrots. Be sure to use an orange-toned base card so that it resembles carrot not chocolate cake. Also try making coffee cake, lemon cake or wedding cake slices.

Christmas Penguin

Materials:

Templates: wing and beak (page 6)

Round papier-mâché box, 5cm (2in)

Red and green striped paper

Black, white, yellow, red and lime green card

White glitter card

Red self-adhesive gemstone

Chalks

All-purpose glue

3D foam pads

Tools:

Circle punch, 5cm (2in)

Oval punch, 5.5 x 3cm (2⅛ x 1¼in)

Tiny hole punch

Holly punch or die

Craft knife and cutting mat

The mini matching gift tag is made in the same way, then mounted on a small folded oval card. Fold your card first, then trim to the oval shape.

Instructions:

1 Cover the sides of the round box with red and green striped paper. Punch a 5cm (2in) circle of red card and glue to the box base. Cut a strip of lime green card to cover the sides of the box lid.

2 Cut a 12cm (4¾in) diameter circle from black card and cut in half. Roll into a cone shape overlapping about 3cm (1¼in) at the edge and glue.

3 Punch an oval from white card and trim away at one end to create the double curve at the top of the penguin's face. Punch tiny holes for the eyes and chalk the cheeks.

4 Use the templates to cut two wings from black card and one beak from yellow card. Fold the beak in half and glue in place. Curl the wings and attach to the body cone, then glue the white oval on top.

5 Punch a 5cm (2in) circle from red card, cut in half and glue into a cone shape for the hat. Cut a hatband 0.8 x 8.5cm (½ x 3⅜in) from white glitter card and glue both hat and band to the penguin.

6 Punch or hand-cut a holly leaf from lime green card and glue to the hatband. Add a red gemstone. Apply a line of glue around the top edge of the box lid and glue the penguin in place.

Easter Chick

By using yellow card instead of black the penguin can be easily transformed into an Easter chick. Add a mini bonnet and basket to complete the new identity. Also try a Christmas robin, a blue bird, or even a turkey with the addition of some tail feathers!

Stacking Snowman

Materials:

Templates: arm, mitten and hat crown (page 6)

White, red, lime green, and orange card

Lime green dotty card

Red and green striped card

Silver self-adhesive gemstone

Chalks

All-purpose glue

3D foam pads

Tools:

Circle punches, 2.5cm (1in) and 1.3cm (⅝in)

Holly punch

Cricut machine with 'accent essentials' cartridge or snowflake punch, 5.5cm (2⅛in)

Wavy scissors

Tiny hole punch

Craft knife and cutting mat

Scissors

Instructions:

1 Cut a 21.5cm (8½in) square of white card. Score 8cm (3¼in) from each side, and cut in on one of the score lines on each side, as far as the central square. Fold to create the box sides and tabs.

2 Repeat with a 17.8cm (6⅞in) square of lime green dotty card, scoring 6cm (2¼in) from each edge; a 12cm (4¾in) square of white card, scoring 4cm (1½in) from each edge; and 7.3cm (3in) square of red card, scoring 1.5cm (⅝in) from each edge.

3 Trim the edges of the dotty box shape with wavy scissors and glue the tabs to create the box lid.

4 Punch two 1.3cm (⅝in) circles of white card for the cheeks, colour them with chalk and glue to one side of the small white box. Cut a smile and punch eyes. Roll a cone from quarter of a 2.5cm (1in) circle of orange card and glue in place for the nose.

5 Use the templates to cut two arms from white card and a pair of mittens from red card. Glue together and add pieces of striped card 2.5 x 1cm (1 x ½in) for the cuffs.

6 Glue the tabs to assemble the head box. Glue the arms to the top of the body box and fold slightly so that they hang down, then glue the head in place on the body box covering the shoulder ends of the arms.

7 Cut a strip of striped card 1.5 x 30cm (⅝ x 11¾in) for the scarf. Fringe the ends using scissors and attach around the neck using 3D foam pads. Cut off the ends just below the point where they cross over and reposition them beneath the 'knot' so that they lie neatly.

8 Use the template to create the tapered hat sides and crown. Score where shown, fold on the score lines and glue. Use the red box made in step 2 for the hat brim, and cut a 2.2cm (1⅛in) square hole in the centre of the lid.

9 Push the base tabs of the hat crown through the hole in the hat brim and glue them on the inside. Cut a hatband 1cm (½in) wide from striped card, wrap around the hat and glue.

10 Use a Cricut machine or large punch to create a snowflake. Glue to the back of each of the mittens to hold the arms in place. Add a punched holly leaf to the hat with a self-adhesive gemstone berry.

Winter Warmer

Give our frosty friend a warmer look using homespun colours of burgundy and olive green. This vintage colour scheme works particularly well if you also change the colour of the main body to soft beige. A snowman made in cool blues and purples would look great too.

Acknowledgements

Thanks to the fantastic team at Search Press:
to Roz, Katie, Debbie and Marrianne for
allowing me to indulge my passion for cutting
and sticking fiddly bits once again. Thanks
also to Dad for keeping the builders at bay,
to Mum for keeping Phoebe amused and to
Christian for keeping out of the way!